THE GREAT CANADIAN COLLAPSE

WILL STICKLE

THE GREAT CANADIAN COLLAPSE

CONTENTS

INTRODUCTION: A NATION IN FREEFALL

C anada stands at a precipice. Once a country admired for its stability, prosperity, and freedom, it now finds itself in rapid decline. The cost of living has soared beyond reach for the average citizen, the national debt has ballooned to unfathomable levels, industries that once provided stable jobs are being regulated out of existence, and a growing dependency on government welfare has eroded self-reliance. Every new policy out of Ottawa seems to do more damage than good, but the question remains: Is this an orchestrated collapse, or merely the inevitable result of decades of reckless governance?

The signs of decay are everywhere.

· Housing Crisis: The average home price in Canada has surpassed $700,000, while median household income remains stagnant, making homeownership virtually impossible for younger generations.

· National Debt Explosion: Canada's federal debt has skyrocketed past $1.2 trillion, nearly doubling in the last decade, placing a crushing financial burden on future generations.· Cost of Living: Inflation has driven grocery prices up by over 20% in the past five years, while energy costs continue to rise due to carbon taxes and green policies.

· Industry Decline: Manufacturing output has shrunk by over 25% in the last two decades, while resource sectors like oil and gas have been deliberately strangled by regulatory policies.

· Welfare State Expansion: Government assistance programs have ballooned, with nearly 40% of Canadians now receiving some form of direct government support, fostering economic dependency over self-sufficiency.

· Censorship and Free Speech Erosion: Government legislation on online content regulation and misinformation control has tightened, creating an environment where dissenting voices are systematically silenced.

From the housing market—where homeownership is a distant dream for young Canadians—to the energy sector, which has been deliberately hamstrung by policies dictated by unelected global bureaucrats, the country is unraveling. Public discourse is suffocated by censorship laws under the guise of 'combatting misinformation,' while the very institutions meant to protect democracy seem more interested in maintaining a status quo that serves only the elite.

Yet, despite the overwhelming evidence of decline, there is no consensus on its cause. Are we watching the premeditated dismantling of a once-thriving nation, carefully orchestrated by globalist interests and political elites? Or is this simply what happens when bureaucratic incompetence, ideological dogma, and economic illiteracy collide in an era of increasing government overreach?

In The Great Canadian Collapse: Conspiracy or Chaos?, we will examine the structural failures that have led Canada to this moment. We will analyze the policies that have gutted the middle class, the economic mismanagement that has placed future generations in financial chains, and the cultural shifts that have transformed self-sufficiency into a relic of the past. Most importantly, we will ask the hard questions: If this is a conspiracy, who benefits? And if it is merely chaos, how did it get this bad?

The answers may not be comfortable, but they are necessary. The time for blind optimism and patriotic platitudes has long passed. The question is no longer whether Canada is in trouble—it's whether this decline is reversible, or if the nation is already too far gone.

This book will pull no punches. It will investigate the forces—both internal and external—that have led to the Great Canadian Collapse, and ultimately, it will challenge you, the reader, to decide: Are we witnessing a grand design of destruction, or the unavoidable fallout of a country that simply lost its way?

PART 1: ECONOMIC SABOTAGE OR GROSS MISMANAGEMENT?

Part 1: Economic Sabotage or Gross Mismanagement?

CHAPTER 1: THE DEATH OF THE MIDDLE CLASS

Canada's economy is unraveling, not by accident, but by a series of deliberate choices that have made life harder for its citizens. Inflation has become a permanent fixture, taxation grows unchecked, and economic policies increasingly favor bureaucratic control over individual prosperity. The result? A working-class squeezed from all sides, a middle class vanishing into debt, and a system that no longer rewards effort—only compliance.

Inflation isn't just a number on a chart—it's an unrelenting force stripping Canadians of their ability to build a future. Food prices aren't just high; they're criminal. Essentials like dairy, meat, and vegetables have jumped over 20% in just a few years, yet wages barely move. Homeownership has become a luxury reserved for the politically connected and the elite, while mortgage rates slam the door shut on those trying to enter the market. Energy costs—once a foundation of Canada's economic strength—are now weapons wielded against the working class under the banner of 'green policy.' But let's not pretend this is just some unfortunate economic cycle. It's policy-driven. The printing of billions of dollars, reckless deficit spending, and interest rate manipulations have devalued every dollar in your pocket. The government calls it 'stimulus'—but for whom? Certainly not for the average worker watching their rent skyrocket and their savings evaporate.

Every dollar you make is under siege. Between federal and provincial income taxes, sales tax, carbon taxes, and hidden fees, Canadians are taxed at nearly every point of economic activity. And despite record-breaking tax revenue, the government still claims it needs more. More to mismanage. More to throw into bloated programs that produce nothing. More to send overseas while infrastructure crumbles at home. Owning a home? Taxed. Driving to work? Taxed. Trying to heat your house in the winter? Taxed again. Meanwhile, corporations cozy with Ottawa get bailouts and loopholes, while small businesses suffocate under regulations designed to keep them from competing. The tax burden is no longer about funding a functioning state—it's about control. It's about ensuring that no one but the ruling class can ever truly thrive.

The modern Canadian economy doesn't reward productivity—it punishes it. Those who work hard to build something face endless regulatory hurdles, while those who resign themselves to dependence are handed just enough to stay afloat, never enough to break free. Nearly 40% of Canadians receive some form of direct government assistance. Is that a safety net or an economic leash? At the same time, entire industries are being dismantled. The energy sector—once the backbone of Canada's economy—is shackled by carbon taxes and environmental regulations designed to keep it from competing on a global scale. Manufacturing has been gutted, and small businesses, the real drivers of economic growth, are drowned in bureaucracy. This isn't progress. This is a carefully managed decline.

What's left to say? There is no need for a neat, tidy ending—because this isn't over. It's happening right now. The dollar in your pocket is worth less today than it was yesterday. The taxes you pay aren't making your life better. The rules keep changing, and every change seems to benefit those who write them, not the people who live under them. So is this just the natural decay of a mismanaged system, or is it something more? A restructuring? A redistribution? A deliberate shift toward a society where power is consolidated in the hands of a few while the rest are pacified with just enough to survive, but never enough to challenge the order? Decide for yourself. But don't expect those in charge to fix what they've worked so hard to break.

The Wealth Gap: How Government Intervention Made Home-ownership Impossible

Homeownership was once the cornerstone of middle-class prosperity in Canada, a symbol of financial security and personal achievement. Today, it has become an unattainable dream for an increasing number of Canadians, locked out by a combination of government overreach, reckless economic policies, and a financial system rigged in favor of the wealthy. What was once a straightforward path—work hard, save, and buy a home—has turned into a financial labyrinth where only those with insider advantages can win.

The average home price in Canada has soared past $700,000, with major cities seeing prices well beyond that. Meanwhile, wages have failed to keep pace, leaving an entire generation struggling to afford even a down payment. Decades of monetary manipulation, tax policies that discourage homeownership for the working class, and government intervention that artificially inflates demand have all contributed to a crisis that benefits the few at the expense of the many.

Government-backed policies such as excessive mortgage stress tests, rent controls, and restrictive zoning laws have created artificial barriers to ownership. Instead of promoting affordability, these interventions have further squeezed supply, driving prices even higher. At the same time, foreign investment loopholes, corporate real estate conglomerates, and government incentives for large-scale developers have ensured that the housing market remains a speculative playground rather than a foundation for stable communities.

The Bank of Canada's reckless interest rate manipulations have exacerbated the issue. By keeping rates artificially low for years, they created an environment where easy credit fueled rapid price growth. Then, when inflation spiraled out of control—thanks in part to massive government spending—the sudden rate hikes trapped new homeowners in financial quicksand while doing nothing to alleviate the structural issues in the market. The result? First-time buyers are either priced out entirely or forced into mortgage arrangements that leave them financially vulnerable for decades.

Adding insult to injury, taxation policies disproportionately punish those trying to enter the market while rewarding those who already hold wealth. High property taxes, land transfer taxes, and hidden fees drive up the cost of purchasing and maintaining a home. Meanwhile, government subsidies and incentives aimed at 'affordable housing' initiatives often end up enriching developers while doing little to provide long-term solutions for those in need. The growing disparity in homeownership is not just a product of market forces—it is the direct result of a system designed to concentrate wealth and power. The working class is squeezed out while institutional investors and politically connected elites consolidate their holdings. The government, rather than correcting course, continues to layer on regulations and policies that worsen the crisis, all while pretending to champion affordability.

The question remains: Is this incompetence, or is it deliberate? Is the goal truly to make housing more accessible, or is it to create a permanent renter class, dependent on government programs and locked out of the generational wealth that homeownership once provided? Whatever the answer, one thing is clear—unless something drastic changes, the dream of owning a home will remain just that: a dream.

2: DEBT, WELFARE, AND THE POLITICS OF DEPENDENCY

The expansion of Canada's welfare state has reshaped the nation's economy, workforce, and social structure in ways that are impossible to ignore. Once intended as a safety net for the truly vulnerable, government assistance has ballooned into an entrenched system that fosters dependency, punishes productivity, and erodes personal responsibility. The consequences are dire: a shrinking labor force, skyrocketing government debt, and a population increasingly reliant on state handouts rather than self-sufficiency.

Welfare programs now extend well beyond traditional unemployment insurance or disability support. Today, nearly 40% of Canadians receive some form of direct government assistance, whether through income supplements, housing subsidies, childcare credits, or universal basic income trials. What began as a limited measure to help those in need has transformed into a culture of entitlement, where incentives to work, save, and invest are steadily being replaced by the expectation that the government will provide.

The economic impact is devastating. The welfare state is not funded by unlimited resources; it is financed by taxation, debt, and inflation. As benefits expand, so too do the taxes that fund them. The burden falls hardest on the productive middle class, whose earnings are siphoned away to sustain government programs that offer little in return. High tax rates discourage ambition and innovation, driving entrepreneurs and skilled workers elsewhere while enabling an underclass that remains dependent on perpetual handouts.

The workforce is shrinking as well. With government support often exceeding the wages of low-skilled jobs, many Canadians are choosing not to work at all. Business owners struggle to find employees willing to take on essential roles, forcing them to either automate, hire foreign labor, or shut down entirely. The government's response? More immigration to compensate for a labor shortage it created, further exacerbating housing demand, resource depletion, and cultural friction.

At the heart of the welfare state's expansion is a political strategy—buying votes with taxpayer money. The more people rely on government programs, the more power politicians wield over their lives. Subsidies and direct cash transfers create a population less likely to push back against rising taxation and expanding bureaucracy. A nation built on personal responsibility and ambition is being replaced by one where dependence is the norm and freedom is eroded one policy at a time.

The long-term consequences of this economic model are unsustainable. As government spending balloons, deficits climb higher, and the value of the Canadian dollar diminishes. Inflation surges, eroding the very purchasing power of those the welfare state claims to help. Meanwhile, generational cycles of dependency become entrenched, as children raised in government-subsidized households grow up to expect the same for themselves.

The question is no longer whether Canada can afford this level of welfare spending—it is whether it can survive it. How long before the productive class, taxed into oblivion, stops playing along? How long before the currency collapses under the weight of unsustainable spending? And how long before the very concept of self-reliance becomes a relic of the past? The welfare state was meant to be a last resort, yet it has become a way of life. The consequences of this shift are already evident, but the worst may be yet to come.

Is Canada Following the Weimar Republic Playbook?

History has a way of repeating itself, especially when governments refuse to learn from past mistakes. The Weimar Republic, Germany's failed interwar democracy, collapsed under the weight of runaway debt, reckless money printing, hyperinflation, and societal destabilization. Canada, once a beacon of stability, now seems to be walking a similar path—piling on debt, devaluing its currency, fostering economic dependence, and eroding its social fabric. The question is no longer whether parallels exist but whether the outcome will be the same.

Weimar Germany's economic downfall was triggered by crushing debt, inflationary policies, and an overreliance on short-term government intervention. Canada is on a disturbingly similar trajectory. The national debt has exploded past $1.2 trillion, with no sign of slowing down. Deficit spending continues at unsustainable levels, under the guise of 'stimulating the economy.' But history shows that government spending sprees do not create prosperity—they create inflation, devalue savings, and eventually, destroy confidence in the currency itself.

The most infamous aspect of Weimar Germany's collapse was hyperinflation. At its peak, the German mark became worthless, requiring wheelbarrows of cash to buy basic goods. While Canada has not yet reached such extremes, the warning signs are everywhere. Inflation has surged well beyond official government figures, eroding purchasing power faster than wages can adjust. Essentials like food, housing, and energy have become prohibitively expensive. The Bank of Canada, like its Weimar counterpart, has played a central role—first by keeping interest rates artificially low, then by hiking them aggressively, destabilizing the very markets it claims to regulate.

Another eerie parallel is the breakdown of social cohesion. Weimar Germany was plagued by class warfare, political extremism, and an increasing dependence on state intervention. Canada is witnessing similar divisions. The middle class is being systematically eroded, as the wealth gap widens between those who own assets and those who can no longer afford them. Political discourse has become more polarized, fueled by media manipulation and government narratives that pit citizens against one another. The welfare state has expanded to unsustainable levels, ensuring more Canadians rely on government support rather than personal industry, just as it did in the Weimar years before collapse.

Perhaps the most alarming similarity is the erosion of democracy itself. The Weimar Republic's downfall was hastened by the rise of authoritarianism, as the government resorted to censorship, emergency powers, and suppression of dissent to maintain control. Canada's increasing restrictions on free speech, its crackdown on independent media, and its growing surveillance state all follow a disturbingly familiar script. The government's ability to freeze bank accounts, regulate online content, and control narratives through taxpayer-funded media is a modern parallel to Weimar-era state overreach.

The Weimar Republic did not collapse overnight. It was a slow, grinding process of economic decay, government mismanagement, and a growing disillusionment with the state. Canada is not yet at the breaking point, but it is moving in that direction. If history is any guide, the next stages will involve even more desperate economic interventions, escalating state control, and eventually, a crisis that forces a reckoning.

The only question that remains is whether Canadians will recognize these warning signs in time—or if, like the Weimar citizens before them, they will watch their country unravel, powerless to stop it.

3 - INDUSTRY DESTRUCTION – BY ACCIDENT OR DESIGN?

The War on Energy and Resource Industries

Canada, once a global leader in natural resources, is now sabotaging its own energy sector under the banner of environmentalism and globalist policy mandates. The country sits on an abundance of oil, gas, and other natural resources that should provide economic security and prosperity, yet government intervention, overregulation, and punitive taxation have deliberately strangled the industry. What was once a powerhouse of employment and national wealth has become a political battleground, with elites pushing an agenda that favors dependency on foreign energy while crippling domestic production.

Policies like carbon taxes, emissions caps, and restrictive drilling and pipeline regulations have not only driven investment out of Canada but have also made energy unaffordable for its own citizens. Instead of leveraging its natural advantages, Canada imports oil from nations with far worse environmental and human rights records, all while demonizing its own industry. The contradiction is staggering—shutting down domestic production under the guise of 'climate leadership' while propping up foreign regimes with lower environmental standards.

The carbon tax, which was sold as a means to combat climate change, has done little but drive up the cost of living for ordinary Canadians. Fuel, heating, transportation, and even food prices have all risen as businesses pass these costs onto consumers. At the same time, energy sector workers have been left behind, with thousands of jobs vanishing due to government policies that favor subsidies for unreliable renewables over the stable, job-rich industries that built Canada's economy.

The consequences of this war on energy are widespread. Manufacturing and industry rely on affordable energy to remain competitive, but with skyrocketing costs and regulatory barriers, businesses are moving elsewhere. Rural and Indigenous communities, many of which have traditionally depended on resource extraction for economic survival, are being told they must transition to 'green jobs' that don't exist. Meanwhile, taxpayers are forced to subsidize green energy projects that are neither efficient nor economically viable, creating a boondoggle that benefits corporate cronies while leaving everyday Canadians with higher bills.

Canada's energy policies are not just about the environment—they are about control. By crippling the energy sector, the government increases dependency on state programs and foreign energy sources. This is not a transition; it is an intentional dismantling of national wealth and sovereignty. The cost of this ideological crusade is being paid by Canadians who are forced to choose between heating their homes and putting food on the table, all while watching their nation's vast resources be squandered in the name of globalist commitments.

The path forward is clear—either Canada reclaims its energy independence and re-establishes its position as a resource powerhouse, or it continues down the road of economic servitude, where power is dictated by foreign interests and bureaucratic elites. The choice is not just economic—it is a matter of national survival.

Red Tape and Regulations Crushing Small Businesses

Small businesses have long been the backbone of Canada's economy, creating jobs, fostering innovation, and driving local prosperity. Yet in recent years, government regulations, excessive taxation, and bureaucratic red tape have systematically suffocated these enterprises. While large corporations benefit from political connections, subsidies, and loopholes, small businesses are being crushed under the weight of compliance costs, labor laws, and ever-changing mandates that favor centralized control over free-market competition.

The regulatory burden on small businesses has reached absurd levels. Entrepreneurs are forced to navigate a labyrinth of permits, zoning laws, environmental regulations, and labor codes before they can even open their doors. Once in operation, they face a constant barrage of tax filings, licensing fees, workplace compliance measures, and bureaucratic audits that consume both time and capital. The sheer complexity of these requirements discourages entrepreneurship, leaving market opportunities increasingly in the hands of multinational corporations that have the legal teams and financial clout to absorb the cost of doing business under a crushing regulatory regime.

The tax system is another mechanism used to squeeze small businesses into submission. Corporate tax rates disproportionately affect independent businesses, while multinational firms exploit offshore tax havens and government loopholes. Payroll taxes, provincial business taxes, and hidden fees add to the burden, forcing many owners to cut jobs, reduce hours, or shut down entirely. The COVID-19 era amplified this divide, where lockdowns and emergency measures disproportionately targeted small businesses while big-box retailers and e-commerce giants thrived under government-sanctioned monopolies.

Employment laws are another hurdle that small business owners struggle to clear. Minimum wage hikes, mandatory benefits, and strict labor codes—though well-intended in theory—often make it impossible for small enterprises to compete. These measures disproportionately benefit large corporations, which can auto-mate jobs or outsource labor, while small businesses are left with no choice but to cut staff or close up shop. Government-man-dated hiring policies further complicate operations, making it harder for businesses to employ based on merit and economic necessity rather than state-imposed quotas and compliance rules.

Perhaps most insidious is the use of environmental and social governance (ESG) mandates to force compliance with globalist corporate policies that have nothing to do with business viability. Small businesses are now expected to implement sustainability measures, diversity programs, and carbon reporting, which im-pose costs that only large firms can absorb. This is not about protecting the environment or promoting equity—it is about con-solidating market power into the hands of those who are aligned with the state's agenda.

The result of this regulatory war on small businesses is clear: fewer startups, fewer opportunities for economic independence, and a greater shift toward centralized, corporate-dominated mar-kets. The middle class, once built on entrepreneurial success, is being eradicated in favor of a model where only massive corpora-tions with government ties can survive. This is not an accident; it is an intentional restructuring of the economy, where free-mar-ket competition is replaced with a controlled economy dictated by policy rather than innovation.

Unless Canada reverses course, entrepreneurship will become a relic of the past, and the only 'businesses' left standing will be those that have pledged allegiance to the bureaucratic elite. The consequences will be devastating—not just economically, but socially, as independence and self-sufficiency are systematically replaced with dependence and subservience.

Who Benefits from Canada's Deindustrialization?

Canada's once-thriving industrial sector has been systematically dismantled through excessive regulation, globalist trade agreements, and policies that prioritize foreign interests over domestic productivity. Factories have shut down, resource extraction has been crippled, and manufacturing has been outsourced to countries with lower labor costs and fewer environmental restrictions. The result? A weakened economy, skyrocketing unemployment in key sectors, and a growing dependence on imports for goods that were once produced domestically. The question that must be asked is—who benefits from Canada's deindustrialization?

The primary winners of this economic shift are globalist corporations and foreign nations that now dominate the markets Canada once controlled. Multinational companies, unburdened by local labor laws, environmental standards, and corporate tax rates, have found it far more profitable to offshore production while still selling their goods at inflated prices in Canada. Instead of producing steel, automobiles, or consumer electronics domestically, Canada has become a passive market for foreign-made goods, erasing high-paying industrial jobs and replacing them with low-wage service sector positions.

China is one of the biggest beneficiaries of Canada's deindustrialization. As domestic manufacturing has withered under the weight of environmental restrictions, carbon taxes, and trade deals that undermine competitiveness, China has filled the gap, flooding the market with cheap, government-subsidized products. Canadian workers are left unemployed while a communist regime exploits its state-controlled economy to expand its global influence. The government, rather than pushing for domestic revitalization, has instead embraced policies that deepen this economic reliance, allowing Canada to become little more than a consumer colony for foreign production.

Financial elites and investment firms also stand to gain from deindustrialization. As traditional industries collapse, their assets are scooped up at bargain prices, repurposed for speculative investments, or turned into greenwashing projects that yield government subsidies. Institutional investors and corporate oligarchs have no stake in Canadian industrial independence; their wealth grows regardless of whether Canada produces anything of real value, as long as money keeps flowing through controlled financial markets.

One of the key figures in Canada's economic trajectory is Mark Carney, former Governor of the Bank of Canada and the Bank of England, and a major architect of the globalist economic policies that have contributed to deindustrialization. Carney has positioned himself as a champion of 'green finance' and ESG investment, pushing policies that cripple traditional industries like oil, gas, and manufacturing while funneling capital into speculative climate-based financial markets. His advocacy for carbon taxes, aggressive monetary policy, and a transition away from resource-based wealth aligns with the same globalist agenda that benefits multinational corporations while leaving working-class Canadians behind.

Carney's influence extends beyond monetary policy. As a key figure within organizations like the World Economic Forum (WEF) and an outspoken proponent of the Great Reset, he has played a direct role in shaping policies that prioritize economic control over national prosperity. His push for financial institutions to divest from fossil fuels and traditional energy sources has accelerated the decline of Canada's industrial base, further increasing reliance on imported goods and foreign energy. While Carney positions himself as a thought leader on economic transformation, the reality is that his policies have disproportionately harmed Canadian workers, stripping away opportunities in favor of a centralized, technocratic economic model.

Government bureaucracies and political elites profit as well. With each new regulatory measure, each new carbon tax, and each new free trade deal that benefits international interests over domestic industry, they consolidate more power. Their ability to control economic activity increases, as businesses must seek state approval, grants, or tax incentives just to remain competitive. The more the government crushes industry, the more dependent companies become on political favor, ensuring that decision-making remains in the hands of bureaucrats rather than market forces.

The losers in all of this are, as always, the working and middle classes. Towns built around manufacturing and resource extraction have been hollowed out, leaving communities to decay while foreign-made goods flood store shelves. Small businesses that relied on industrial production have shuttered. The skilled trades, once a pathway to financial independence and stability, are disappearing as economic policies push young people toward debt-ridden university degrees instead of high-paying industrial jobs that no longer exist.

Canada's deindustrialization is not a coincidence—it is the result of a calculated shift in policy that favors globalism, corporate monopolies, and political control over national prosperity. Those at the top benefit from a system that prioritizes financial speculation over real production, while the average citizen is left to navigate an economy that produces less, costs more, and offers fewer opportunities for economic independence. The only way to reverse this trend is to restore the conditions that allow industry to thrive—by cutting red tape, restoring domestic energy production, and rejecting the economic policies that have turned Canada into a resource-rich country incapable of sustaining its own industrial base.

PART 2: THE CULTURAL AND POLITICAL COLLAPSE

P art 2: The Cultural and Political Collapse

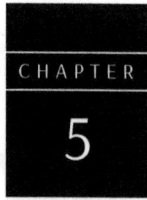

4: IMMIGRATION AS A TOOL OF ECONOMIC MANIPULATION

I s Mass Immigration Solving or Worsening the Crisis?
Mass immigration has long been promoted as a solution to Canada's economic and demographic challenges. The official narrative insists that an aging population, declining birth rates, and labor shortages necessitate a high influx of newcomers to sustain growth and fund social programs. Yet, as immigration numbers continue to hit record highs, the cracks in this argument have become impossible to ignore. Far from solving Canada's economic woes, mass immigration is exacerbating the very crises it was meant to fix—driving up housing prices, overwhelming public services, suppressing wages, and fueling social fragmentation.

The housing market is the most obvious casualty. With Canada accepting over 500,000 new permanent residents annually, not including temporary workers and international students, the demand for housing has far outstripped supply. The result has been skyrocketing home prices and rental costs that push both new-comers and existing Canadians into financial hardship. Politicians deflect blame onto 'market forces' and 'supply chain issues,' yet the reality is simple: when millions of people are added to a system already at capacity, affordability becomes a pipe dream for the working and middle classes.

Public services are also buckling under the strain. Schools, hospitals, and transportation networks were struggling before record immigration levels, and now, they are reaching breaking points. Emergency rooms are overwhelmed, classrooms are overcrowded, and infrastructure development has failed to keep pace with population growth. Instead of easing demographic pressures, mass immigration has made it impossible to sustain the quality of life Canadians once enjoyed.

The labor market argument—the claim that immigrants are needed to fill job shortages—doesn't hold up under scrutiny. While some industries do face labor shortages, mass immigration often suppresses wages by increasing competition for low and middle-income jobs. Employers benefit from a surplus of workers willing to accept lower wages, but native-born Canadians and earlier immigrants suffer the consequences. The government's response has been to flood the workforce with temporary foreign workers and low-skilled laborers, creating an underclass of workers who have little path to economic mobility while driving wages down across the board.

Another overlooked consequence is the cultural and social impact of rapid demographic shifts. While Canada has a history of successful immigration, the scale and pace of current migration levels are unprecedented. Communities are struggling to integrate new arrivals, social cohesion is fraying, and political tensions are rising. Instead of a controlled, sustainable approach to immigration, the country is engaged in a reckless social experiment where the effects are being felt in rising crime rates, strained social services, and increasing divisions within society.

If mass immigration were truly an economic necessity, why do the costs seem to outweigh the benefits? Why are Canadians poorer, less secure, and more divided than ever before? The answer lies in who actually benefits from the current system. Large corporations, real estate developers, and financial institutions profit enormously from a never-ending influx of new consumers and cheap labor. The government, too, benefits by using immigration as a distraction from its economic failures, portraying it as a panacea for problems it has no real plan to fix.

At current levels, immigration is not solving Canada's economic crisis—it is accelerating it. A country with strained resources, unaffordable housing, and declining job prospects does not need more people to prop up a broken system; it needs leadership willing to address the root causes of these problems. Until Canada prioritizes its existing citizens—ensuring affordable housing, well-paying jobs, and functional public services—the promise that mass immigration will 'save the economy' will remain nothing more than a convenient illusion.

5: CENSORSHIP, MEDIA CONTROL, AND NARRATIVE MANAGE

Trudeau's Online Censorship Laws and the Erosion of Free Speech

Canada has long prided itself on being a democracy that values free expression, open debate, and press freedom. Yet, under the leadership of Justin Trudeau, these fundamental rights have been systematically eroded through a series of online censorship laws designed to silence dissent, control narratives, and grant the government unprecedented authority over digital content. While these measures are often framed as necessary tools to combat 'hate speech,' 'misinformation,' and 'online harms,' the reality is far more sinister—they represent a coordinated effort to restrict free speech, regulate independent media, and shape public discourse to align with the government's ideological agenda.

One of the most controversial laws in this campaign against free expression is Bill C-11, the Online Streaming Act. Marketed as a way to promote Canadian content and level the playing field between traditional broadcasters and digital platforms, this legislation instead hands sweeping powers to the Canadian Radio-television and Telecommunications Commission (CRTC) to regulate online content. While the government insists that C-11 will not affect user-generated content, its vague language and broad scope leave the door open for state control over what Canadians can see, say, and share online.

Even more concerning is Bill C-18, the Online News Act, which forces tech companies like Google and Meta to pay Canadian media outlets for news content. While framed as a move to support journalism, the law effectively funnels money into government-friendly legacy media while crushing independent outlets that challenge the establishment. The result? A heavily curated news ecosystem where only state-approved narratives are amplified, while dissenting voices are buried by algorithmic suppression or financial starvation.

But perhaps the most blatant assault on free speech comes in the form of proposed 'Online Harms' legislation, which seeks to criminalize broad categories of speech under the guise of preventing hate and extremism. The law would require social media platforms to proactively remove 'harmful content' within 24 hours or face massive fines. Who decides what qualifies as 'harmful'? A government-appointed regulatory body, granting the state unchecked power to censor political opposition, satire, investigative journalism, and even private conversations. This is not about protecting Canadians; it is about ensuring that those in power remain unchallenged.

Trudeau's administration has also weaponized financial deplatforming as a tool of censorship. The government's response to the Freedom Convoy protests in 2022 set a chilling precedent when it invoked the Emergencies Act to freeze the bank accounts of protesters and donors without due process. This was not about

preventing economic crime—it was about punishing political opposition and intimidating citizens who dared to question government policies. Today, the infrastructure for financial suppression
remains in place, a constant reminder that in Trudeau's Canada,
dissent carries not just social but economic consequences.

These laws and policies are not happening in isolation—they are
part of a broader global trend where governments seek to regulate
and control online discourse under the pretense of 'safety' and
'responsibility.' The difference is that Canada, once a champion
of civil liberties, is now leading the charge toward a controlled information state. The result is an environment where Canadians
are less free to express themselves, independent media is suffocated, and the government's grip over public discourse tightens
with each passing day.

Free speech is not a privilege granted by the state—it is a fundamental right. Yet, Trudeau's government has made it clear that it
sees this right as a threat to its authority. The only question now
is how much further they will go before the ability to push back
is lost entirely.

Legacy Media and the State's Stranglehold on Public Perception

The Canadian government's grip on public perception is not just
a byproduct of policy—it is an intentional and well-coordinated
effort carried out through a compliant, state-funded media apparatus. What was once an industry tasked with holding power
accountable has devolved into an extension of the government
itself, ensuring that only state-approved narratives dominate the
national discourse. Legacy media, instead of serving as a watch-
dog for the people, has become the government's primary tool for
controlling public opinion, silencing dissent, and manufacturing
consent.

At the heart of this system is the massive financial dependence
of Canadian media on government subsidies. Programs such as

the $600 million media bailout fund and direct tax incentives for 'qualified journalism organizations' ensure that major outlets remain beholden to the same politicians they are supposed to scrutinize. When media companies rely on government handouts to stay afloat, true investigative journalism is replaced by propaganda. Instead of challenging the establishment, reporters become stenographers for the regime, regurgitating talking points that align with official policy while branding dissenters as extremists or conspiracy theorists.

The stranglehold tightens further through legislation like Bill C-18, the Online News Act, which forces tech companies to pay Canadian news organizations for sharing their content. While framed as a way to 'save journalism,' the law is effectively a financial lifeline for legacy media, ensuring their continued survival at the expense of independent and alternative voices. Rather than competing in a free market of ideas, these media outlets are propped up by government intervention, guaranteeing that only their narratives remain dominant.

The result is a media landscape where dissent is marginalized and alternative viewpoints are discredited. Stories that challenge government policies on immigration, economic mismanagement, COVID-19 mandates, or foreign influence are either underreported or framed in a way that ridicules critics. Independent media outlets that do expose uncomfortable truths find themselves demonetized, deplatformed, or algorithmically suppressed, as seen with the increasing censorship of non-mainstream news sources on platforms like YouTube, Facebook, and Google.

The effects of this controlled media environment are profound. Public trust in legacy outlets has plummeted, as more Canadians recognize that they are being fed sanitized, government-approved narratives rather than objective reporting. Yet, despite this decline in credibility, these institutions remain the primary information sources for millions, shaping public opinion through a relentless cycle of selective reporting, omission, and ideological bias.

This is not journalism—it is state-sponsored information control. In a functioning democracy, the media is supposed to challenge those in power, not serve as their public relations arm. But in Canada today, legacy media operates less like an independent press and more like an instrument of propaganda, ensuring that the ruling class maintains control over the national conversation while dissenting voices are silenced or ridiculed.

The state-media complex represents one of the greatest threats to freedom in Canada. Without an independent press, the government is free to rewrite reality, dictate acceptable discourse, and manufacture consent for policies that harm the very citizens they claim to serve. Until this system is dismantled, Canadians will continue to be misled, manipulated, and kept in the dark about the true forces shaping their country's decline.

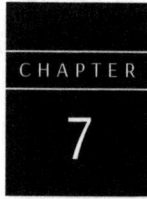

6: A NATION WITHOUT LEADERSHIP

H ow Each Political Party Contributes to the Problem
Canada's decline is not the fault of one leader, one government, or one party—it is the result of a systemic failure across the entire political spectrum. While politicians on all sides claim to offer solutions, the reality is that every major party has contributed to the erosion of economic freedom, national sovereignty, and individual rights. The difference is only in style, not substance. The country lurches from one administration to another, but the fundamental problems remain, because no party has the courage—or the political will—to challenge the system that keeps them in power.

The Liberal Party, under Justin Trudeau, has taken government overreach to new extremes. Expanding the welfare state, driving record levels of immigration without regard for infrastructure, implementing carbon taxes that strangle industry, and pushing censorship laws under the guise of 'protecting democracy,' the Liberals have built a system of dependency and centralized control. Their policies prioritize ideological purity over economic reality, punishing business owners, taxpayers, and anyone who dares to question the narrative. They have perfected the art of identity politics, dividing Canadians into increasingly smaller and more easily controlled factions, while handing out massive subsidies to media and corporate allies to maintain the illusion of public support.

The Conservative Party, despite its rhetoric, has proven to be little more than a controlled opposition force. While it criticizes Liberal policies, it rarely offers a meaningful alternative. Under successive leaders, the Conservatives have failed to reverse big-government policies, failing to repeal draconian laws or cut spending even when in power. They adopt the language of freedom and fiscal responsibility during election cycles, only to compromise once they reach office. At best, they serve as a slightly slower-moving vehicle toward the same globalist economic and social policies that the Liberals embrace. At worst, they serve as a pressure valve, giving Canadians the illusion of choice while maintaining the same bureaucratic, technocratic state.

The New Democratic Party (NDP) has long positioned itself as the champion of workers and social justice, but in reality, it has helped entrench the very economic policies that have made life unaffordable for the working class. Their unwavering support for increased taxation, reckless social spending, and radical progressive policies ensures that government dependence continues to grow. Instead of promoting true economic empowerment, the NDP actively discourages self-reliance, pushing policies that penalize success while rewarding complacency. Their alliance with the Liberals in recent years has made it clear that they exist not to challenge the system, but to ensure that leftist ideology remains dominant in Canadian politics.

The Bloc Québécois, while focusing largely on Quebec nationalism, has played a role in Canada's larger decline by leveraging its political influence to extract financial concessions for Quebec while contributing little to a cohesive national vision. Their existence highlights the deep fractures within Canada, where regional interests trump national unity, and federal policies are often dictated by the need to appease Quebec rather than serve the entire country's interests.

The Green Party, while largely irrelevant in terms of parliamentary influence, has served as an ideological trojan horse for extreme environmental policies that mainstream parties have adopted. Their radical approach to climate policy has provided political cover for policies that destroy domestic energy production, increase the cost of living, and further entrench globalist economic controls under the guise of sustainability.

Even the People's Party of Canada (PPC), which claims to be the only alternative to the establishment, has struggled to gain meaningful traction. While it raises important issues—such as rejecting mass immigration, advocating for free speech, and opposing government overreach—it remains sidelined by a political system designed to suppress dissenting movements outside of the established parties.

No matter who is in power, the fundamental trajectory remains the same: more government control, more debt, more foreign influence, and less economic opportunity for Canadians. Whether it's the Liberals pushing full-speed toward centralized authoritarianism, the Conservatives failing to act as a meaningful counterbalance, or the NDP ensuring that socialist policies remain at the heart of Canadian governance, the political class as a whole benefits from the status quo while the average citizen suffers.

The illusion of choice is one of the greatest tricks in modern democracy. Until Canadians demand a real alternative—one that prioritizes national interests over globalist agendas, economic independence over government dependency, and free speech over state-controlled narratives—nothing will change. The country will continue down the same path, with different faces in charge but the same policies driving it toward collapse.

Is Canada Even a Democracy Anymore, or Just a Corporate-Controlled State?

Canada presents itself as a democratic nation, but beneath the surface, it increasingly resembles a corporate-controlled state where political decisions serve the interests of elites rather than the people. The democratic institutions that once functioned as a check on government power—parliament, the judiciary, the free press—have been steadily co-opted by corporate interests, globalist agendas, and a bureaucracy that operates independently of public accountability. Elections occur, but they change little. Policy decisions that shape the country's economic and social landscape seem to be dictated not by voters but by a well-connected class of business moguls, financial elites, and unelected bureaucrats.

At the core of Canada's democratic decline is the stranglehold that corporations and international organizations have on its policies. The World Economic Forum (WEF), United Nations (UN), and other transnational institutions exert an outsized influence on domestic legislation, pushing policies that prioritize climate activism, mass immigration, digital ID systems, and economic restructuring under the banner of sustainability and inclusivity. These agendas are rarely debated in Parliament or put to a public vote—rather, they are quietly implemented by governments that claim to be acting in the national interest while serving foreign interests instead.

Corporate monopolies have also secured an unprecedented level of control over public policy. Whether in banking, technology, or media, a handful of powerful companies shape the flow of information and economic opportunity. The Big Five banks dictate financial policy, social media platforms regulate speech and political discourse, and legacy media—funded by government subsidies—manufactures consent for policies that benefit the elite at the expense of ordinary citizens. The result is a system where Canadians are increasingly told what they can say, what they can think, and how they must live, all while being convinced that they still have a say in their governance.

The role of government in this transformation cannot be overstated. Ottawa, rather than functioning as an independent governing body accountable to voters, has become a middleman between corporate interests and international policy-making organizations. The carbon tax, which enriches financial markets through emissions trading while punishing working-class Canadians, is a prime example of how policy is crafted to serve economic elites rather than the people. Mass immigration, touted as an economic necessity, ensures a steady supply of cheap labor to keep wages down and boost corporate profits, while the resulting housing crisis prices Canadians out of their own communities. Meanwhile, public infrastructure continues to decay, healthcare systems crumble, and citizens face ever-increasing taxation to sustain a bloated bureaucratic state that delivers little in return.

Perhaps the greatest indication that democracy is failing in Canada is the increasing criminalization of dissent. Free speech is no longer protected; laws such as Bill C-11, Bill C-18, and upcoming 'online harms' legislation enable the government to regulate and censor digital content under the guise of combating misinformation. Protests against government overreach, such as the Freedom Convoy, were met not with dialogue but with financial deplatforming, police crackdowns, and draconian emergency powers that bypassed democratic processes entirely.

Elections themselves are little more than an illusion of choice. The major political parties, despite their rhetoric, operate within the same framework of expanding government control, growing corporate influence, and aligning with globalist objectives. Voter turnout declines with each passing election as more Canadians realize that no matter who they vote for, the system remains the same. Public trust in democracy is collapsing, yet those in power seem more concerned with maintaining control than addressing the grievances of their citizens.

So, is Canada still a democracy? If democracy is defined by free and fair elections, independent institutions, and government accountability to the people, then the answer is increasingly no. Canada today functions more like a corporate state, where policy is dictated by financial elites, multinational corporations, and globalist organizations rather than by the will of the people. If this trajectory continues, the question will not be whether Canada is still a democracy, but whether it ever will be again.

PART 3: CONSPIRACY OR CHAOS?

Part 3: Conspiracy or Chaos? The Case for and Against

7: IF IT'S A CONSPIRACY, WHO BENEFITS?

The WEF, UN, and Foreign Influence on Canadian Policy
Canada's sovereignty is increasingly being compromised by the influence of global organizations like the World Economic Forum (WEF), the United Nations (UN), and foreign corporate interests that dictate policy from behind the scenes. While these institutions claim to act in the best interest of humanity—advocating for climate action, economic equality, and global cooperation—their policies consistently undermine national autonomy, erode democratic decision-making, and prioritize international agendas over the well-being of Canadian citizens.

The WEF, led by Klaus Schwab, openly boasts about its infiltration of national governments, with Canadian politicians—including Justin Trudeau and Chrystia Freeland—closely aligned with the organization's objectives. The WEF's Great Reset agenda is not a conspiracy theory; it is a well-documented plan to reshape economies, transition away from traditional industries, and enforce globalist governance through economic policies like ESG

(Environmental, Social, and Governance) scoring, digital currencies, and carbon credit systems. Many of Canada's economic and
environmental policies, including carbon taxation and aggressive
'green transition' measures, align seamlessly with WEF objectives—often at the expense of Canadian workers, industries, and
energy independence.

The UN plays a similar role, exerting pressure through agreements such as the UN Sustainable Development Goals (SDGs) and
Agenda 2030. These frameworks are presented as guiding principles for global prosperity, but in practice, they serve as mechanisms to impose international regulations on domestic policies,
bypassing democratic debate. From mass immigration targets set
by the UN's Global Compact for Migration to climate policies that
force Canada to restrict its resource sector while other nations
expand theirs, the UN's influence ensures that Canadian governance aligns with global priorities rather than national interests. The government frequently justifies radical policy shifts by
pointing to these agreements, despite the fact that they were
never put to a public vote.

Foreign corporate influence compounds this issue. Multinational
banks, tech giants, and foreign-owned investment firms wield
enormous control over Canadian policy decisions. BlackRock,
Vanguard, and other global financial powerhouses hold major
stakes in Canada's largest corporations, exerting influence over
economic policy, housing markets, and regulatory frameworks.
The push for ESG compliance, which forces companies to adhere
to politically driven environmental and social standards, is a direct result of pressure from these financial institutions. As a result, Canadian industries are strangled by regulations that serve
the interests of global investors rather than national prosperity.

The consequences of this foreign influence are devastating. Policies dictated by the WEF and UN have led to the deindustrialization of Canada, skyrocketing energy costs, mass immigration

without infrastructure planning, and an increasingly digital surveillance state that erodes personal freedoms. Every new global agreement Canada signs weakens its ability to govern independently, reducing elected officials to mere administrators of international directives rather than representatives of their constituents.

Canadians were never given a choice in this transformation. These policies were never put to a referendum, never debated honestly in Parliament, and never presented as campaign issues. Instead, they were quietly implemented through backdoor agreements, corporate lobbying, and bureaucratic maneuvering.

The fundamental question is this: who does the Canadian government truly serve? If decisions are made not by the electorate but by global elites and foreign entities, can Canada even be considered a sovereign nation anymore? Until Canadians reclaim control over their own policies and reject governance by unelected international bodies, the country will continue down a path where its laws, economy, and freedoms are dictated by foreign interests rather than by the people who live within its borders.

Who Profits from Economic Instability and Dependency?

Economic instability is not just a consequence of bad policy—it is a lucrative business model for the elites who profit from crisis and dependency. While the average Canadian struggles with rising costs, job insecurity, and an overburdened welfare state, a select group of corporate, financial, and political interests reap the rewards. The cycle of manufactured instability ensures that wealth and power remain concentrated at the top, while the working and middle classes are kept in a state of permanent struggle.

The financial sector stands to gain the most from economic instability. Central banks, including the Bank of Canada, manipulate interest rates and control the money supply in ways that benefit the banking elite while impoverishing ordinary citizens. Inflation—caused largely by government overspending and monetary expansion—erodes the value of wages and savings, forcing more people into debt just to survive. Who profits from this? Big banks and global investment firms like BlackRock and Vanguard, which thrive on lending money at inflated interest rates and buying up assets when individuals and small businesses are forced to sell.

Multinational corporations also capitalize on economic hardship. As small businesses are crushed by taxation, overregulation, and shifting market conditions, corporate monopolies consolidate their power. The collapse of local competitors ensures that industries—from agriculture to real estate to retail—are controlled by a handful of massive firms that dictate prices, wages, and supply chains. Government policies that claim to 'level the playing field' through subsidies and corporate welfare only serve to strengthen these monopolies, ensuring that economic power remains in the hands of the few.

The welfare state, far from being a safety net, is another tool for control. The more Canadians rely on government handouts—whether through basic income programs, housing subsidies, or employment insurance—the more leverage the state has over its citizens. Dependency is power. Politicians use welfare expansion to secure votes, creating a cycle where the population becomes increasingly reliant on state assistance rather than independent economic success. At the same time, higher taxation on the productive class ensures that those who work the hardest shoulder the financial burden for an expanding class of dependents.

Foreign investors and globalist organizations benefit immensely from a weakened Canadian economy. When instability drives down property values and business assets, international buyers swoop in to purchase prime real estate, farmland, and industries at bargain prices. The result is a country where fewer Canadians own their own homes, businesses, or resources, and more of the nation's wealth is funneled into foreign hands. Policies that encourage mass immigration without proper infrastructure planning serve to increase housing demand, further pricing out native-born Canadians while enriching developers and corporate landlords.

Meanwhile, the political class profits not just financially, but through increased control. An economically desperate population is easier to govern. The less financially secure people are, the less time they have to engage in political resistance or demand accountability from their leaders. By fostering economic instability—through reckless spending, overregulation, and a devalued currency—politicians ensure that they remain the gatekeepers of economic survival, able to sell government intervention as the only solution to the very problems they created.

Economic instability is not a failure of the system; it is the system. Every crisis, every inflationary spike, every financial downturn is an opportunity for the elite to consolidate more wealth, more property, and more control. Until Canadians recognize that economic hardship is not an accident but a feature of the modern power structure, they will remain trapped in a cycle designed to keep them dependent, struggling, and ultimately powerless.

8: IF IT'S JUST CHAOS, HOW DID IT GET THIS BAD?

Bureaucratic Incompetence and the Inevitability of Corruption Canada's bloated bureaucracy is not just inefficient—it is a breeding ground for corruption, waste, and systemic failure. Government agencies, once tasked with serving the public, now exist primarily to sustain themselves, expanding their budgets, increasing their regulatory power, and ensuring that no real accountability ever takes place. The larger and more complex a bureaucracy becomes, the more inevitable its incompetence and corruption. Canada is no exception.

Bureaucracy thrives on inefficiency. Every layer of government—federal, provincial, and municipal—adds more rules, more paperwork, and more red tape, slowing down processes and creating costly obstacles for businesses and individuals. Public sector spending continues to rise, yet services deteriorate. Hospitals are understaffed, infrastructure is crumbling, and wait times for essential services grow longer, but government employees continue to receive pay raises, bonuses, and pension increases. The system is designed to grow itself, not to solve problems.

This self-preserving mechanism creates an environment where corruption is inevitable. The more complex a system, the easier it becomes to hide inefficiencies, misallocated funds, and outright fraud. Billions disappear into government programs with little to no oversight. Departments responsible for managing the economy, healthcare, immigration, and public safety operate with near-total immunity from consequences. When failures occur, bureaucrats simply pass the blame, commission expensive 'studies,' and demand more funding as the solution.

Meanwhile, public contracts are handed out to well-connected firms without competition or transparency. The revolving door between government agencies and the private sector ensures that former bureaucrats transition seamlessly into lucrative corporate positions, using their insider knowledge and political connections to further entrench a system that benefits the elite at the expense of taxpayers. Scandals emerge, but resignations are rare. Accountability is a public relations exercise, not a function of governance.

Regulatory agencies, instead of acting as safeguards, become instruments of control, punishing small businesses while allowing politically favored corporations to bypass restrictions. Environmental regulations destroy Canadian industry while foreign-owned enterprises are given exemptions. Tax authorities relentlessly pursue individuals while multinational companies legally exploit loopholes to avoid paying their fair share. The rules exist not to ensure fairness, but to concentrate power.

The public sector has become a massive, self-sustaining entity with no incentive to reform. Politicians campaign on promises to cut waste, but once in office, they realize that the bureaucracy is too entrenched to dismantle. The people who benefit from this system—the bureaucrats, lobbyists, consultants, and career politicians—have every reason to maintain the status quo, while ordinary Canadians are left to deal with the consequences.

At its core, bureaucratic incompetence is not a flaw—it is the inevitable outcome of unchecked government expansion. Corruption does not occur in spite of the system; it occurs because of it. Without a radical restructuring of governance, the waste, inefficiency, and corruption that define Canada's bureaucratic class will only continue to grow, consuming more resources and delivering less in return. The real question is not whether the system can be fixed, but whether those in power will ever allow it to be.

The Slow Decay of a Nation That Simply Lost Its Way

Nations do not collapse overnight. They erode slowly, piece by piece, as foundational values are abandoned, institutions rot from within, and the will of the people is replaced by complacency, corruption, and state control. Canada is not in the throes of a dramatic revolution or a sudden coup—it is experiencing the kind of gradual decline that is far more insidious, a slow-motion unraveling of a nation that once stood for self-reliance, prosperity, and freedom.

Decades of political mismanagement have dulled the country's economic engine. Where Canada once thrived on its natural resources, manufacturing strength, and a spirit of entrepreneurial independence, it now operates under the weight of crushing taxation, strangling regulation, and a government that sees its own citizens as obstacles rather than stakeholders. The energy sector, once the backbone of the economy, has been systematically dismantled, not by market forces, but by ideological warfare. The housing market, once a vehicle for middle-class stability, has been turned into a speculative racket that benefits foreign investors and financial elites while pricing Canadians out of their own communities.

Culturally, Canada has lost its sense of identity. The rugged individualism and self-reliance that built the nation have been replaced by a culture of dependency, where government handouts are seen as a birthright and personal responsibility is an outdated concept. Free speech, once a pillar of Canadian democracy, is now subject to government regulation, censorship laws, and corporate-enforced social engineering. The media, rather than challenging power, has become a state-funded megaphone, reinforcing the narrative that obedience is a virtue and dissent is dangerous.

Perhaps the most glaring sign of national decay is the loss of confidence in the future. Younger generations, burdened with debt and shut out of meaningful economic opportunity, no longer believe in the Canadian Dream. Immigration, once a tool for measured national growth, has been weaponized into a chaotic mass influx that overwhelms infrastructure and drives down wages, creating an underclass of both new arrivals and native-born Canadians who cannot get ahead. The country is filling up with people, but it is emptying of purpose.

This is how nations die—not with a single catastrophic event, but with an accumulation of betrayals, miscalculations, and policy failures that, over time, corrode everything that once made them great. The decay of Canada is not an accident; it is the result of decades of drift, where those in power prioritized globalist interests, short-term political gains, and bureaucratic expansion over the long-term well-being of their own people.

The only question that remains is whether this decline is reversible. Can a country that has abandoned its founding principles find its way back? Or is this simply the natural consequence of a society that, through complacency and manipulation, has been led so far off course that recovery is no longer an option? History has seen this pattern before, and it has rarely ended in renewal. But if there is any hope left, it lies not in the institutions that failed the nation, but in the individuals who refuse to accept its downfall as inevitable.

9: THE EDUCATION SYSTEM AS AN INDOCTRINATION TOOL

H ow Public Schools and Universities Are Used to Enforce Government Narratives

Education was once about equipping students with knowledge, critical thinking skills, and the ability to engage in free and open debate. Today, Canada's education system has been transformed into an ideological training ground where government narratives are reinforced, dissent is discouraged, and independent thought is replaced with compliance. Public schools and universities, rather than being spaces for intellectual growth, now function as mechanisms for social engineering, ensuring that each new generation is conditioned to accept state-approved perspectives without question.

From an early age, Canadian students are immersed in curricula that emphasize globalist priorities, progressive politics, and government dependency over historical accuracy, personal responsibility, and self-sufficiency. Traditional subjects like history and economics have been rewritten to fit modern ideological frameworks, downplaying Canada's foundational values in favor of narratives that focus on systemic oppression, collective guilt, and the necessity of state intervention in all aspects of life. Rather than producing well-rounded, critical thinkers, the system churns out individuals who reflexively accept government policy as the only solution to societal problems.

The push for identity politics and social justice ideology dominates classrooms, replacing merit-based education with activist-driven curriculums. Concepts like Critical Race Theory (CRT), gender theory, and radical environmentalism are embedded in lessons, not as topics for debate, but as unquestionable truths. Those who push back against these narratives—whether students, teachers, or parents—are often labeled as reactionaries or extremists, creating a chilling effect that discourages open discussion and free inquiry. Dissenting voices are silenced through social pressure, institutional policies, and, in some cases, disciplinary action.

Universities, once bastions of academic freedom, have become even more rigid enforcers of state-sanctioned narratives. Professors who challenge progressive orthodoxy risk losing their jobs or facing public smear campaigns. Speech codes and 'safe spaces' ensure that controversial ideas—especially those critical of government policy—are kept out of the academic sphere. The result is a generation of students who are not taught how to think but what to think, ensuring that the values of self-reliance, national identity, and economic freedom are marginalized while government control is normalized.

The effects of this indoctrination extend beyond the classroom. Graduates emerge from these institutions not as independent thinkers, but as advocates for the very policies that limit their own freedoms. They embrace increased government intervention, wealth redistribution, and censorship laws as necessary tools for progress, unaware that they are simply echoing the talking points they have been fed for years. The ability to critically assess government actions, challenge mainstream narratives, and question authority is systematically eradicated, replaced with blind faith in the institutions that claim to serve them.

Meanwhile, trade schools, independent learning models, and alternative education programs—once viable paths to economic independence—are increasingly devalued in favor of expensive, debt-inducing university degrees that provide little real-world application. This shift ensures that students graduate not only with ideological conformity but also with financial dependency, making them more reliant on government assistance and corporate employment.

Education in Canada is no longer about empowerment—it is about control. By shaping the minds of young Canadians to accept government narratives as absolute truths, the ruling class ensures that its grip on power remains unchallenged. Until education is reclaimed as a tool for independent thought rather than ideological conditioning, the cycle of dependency, compliance, and centralized control will only deepen.

How Public Schools and Universities Are Used to Enforce Government Narratives

Education was once about equipping students with knowledge, critical thinking skills, and the ability to engage in free and open debate. Today, Canada's education system has been transformed into an ideological training ground where government narratives are reinforced, dissent is discouraged, and independent thought is replaced with compliance. Public schools and universities, rather than being spaces for intellectual growth, now function as mechanisms for social engineering, ensuring that each new generation is conditioned to accept state-approved perspectives without question.

From an early age, Canadian students are immersed in curricula that emphasize globalist priorities, progressive politics, and government dependency over historical accuracy, personal responsibility, and self-sufficiency. Traditional subjects like history and economics have been rewritten to fit modern ideological frameworks, downplaying Canada's foundational values in favor of narratives that focus on systemic oppression, collective guilt, and the necessity of state intervention in all aspects of life. Rather than producing well-rounded, critical thinkers, the system churns out individuals who reflexively accept government policy as the only solution to societal problems

The Decline of Critical Thinking and the Rise of Ideological Programming
Critical thinking—the ability to analyze, question, and challenge ideas—has been systematically removed from the modern education system. Instead of teaching students how to think, schools now teach them what to think. Debate and open discourse, once hallmarks of higher education, have been replaced with rigid ideological programming that rewards conformity and punishes dissent.
One of the key strategies in this transformation has been the elimination of classical education models that emphasized logical reasoning, rhetoric, and debate. In their place, subjective and activist-driven content has become the norm. Students are taught that certain perspectives are inherently virtuous while others are dangerous and must be suppressed. Self-censorship is instilled at an early age, ensuring that young Canadians learn to silence their own doubts rather than risk social or academic consequences for challenging prevailing narratives.
The shift is especially evident in the use of "safe spaces" and speech codes on university campuses, where students are discouraged from engaging with ideas that challenge their world-

view. Professors who question mainstream ideologies face social ostracization or professional consequences, while students who deviate from the accepted line are shamed or penalized. Instead of fostering resilience and intellectual rigor, universities now produce individuals who rely on emotional appeals and dogmatic beliefs rather than evidence-based reasoning.

This deliberate suppression of critical thinking is essential for maintaining state control. A population that is unable to question government policies, recognize logical inconsistencies, or demand accountability is far easier to govern. The media, political class, and corporate sector all benefit from an education system that produces obedient workers and compliant voters rather than independent thinkers and problem-solvers.

The effects of this shift are evident in the increasing public acceptance of government overreach, censorship, and economic mismanagement. Citizens, having been conditioned to trust the system rather than question it, accept restrictive policies under the guise of safety and progress. The few who do challenge the status quo are dismissed as radicals or conspiracy theorists, reinforcing the idea that deviation from official narratives is dangerous.

Meanwhile, trade schools, independent learning models, and alternative education programs—once viable paths to economic independence—are increasingly devalued in favor of expensive, debt-inducing university degrees that provide little real-world application. This shift ensures that students graduate not only with ideological conformity but also with financial dependency, making them more reliant on government assistance and corporate employment.

Education in Canada is no longer about empowerment—it is about control. By shaping the minds of young Canadians to accept government narratives as absolute truths, the ruling class ensures that its grip on power remains unchallenged. Until education is reclaimed as a tool for independent thought rather than ideological conditioning, the cycle of dependency, compliance, and centralized control will only deepen.

10: CAN CANADA BE SAVED?

Is There a Path to Reversing the Collapse, or Is the Damage Too Far Gone?

The collapse of a nation is rarely reversed. History tells us that once a country reaches a tipping point—where corruption is systemic, institutions are weaponized against the people, and economic decline is intentional rather than accidental—it is difficult, if not impossible, to restore what was lost. Canada is now at such a crossroads. The question is not whether the country is in decline, but whether there is a way back, or if the damage is irreversible.

For those who still hold hope, the path to reversing Canada's collapse would require a radical departure from the status quo. Incremental reforms will not fix a system that has been designed to entrench power in the hands of bureaucratic elites and globalist interests. The country's trajectory can only be changed by dismantling the very structures that are accelerating its downfall.

Dismantling the Bureaucratic State

THE GREAT CANADIAN COLLAPSE

Canada's government has grown too large, too expensive, and too intrusive. Cutting government size, slashing regulations, and eliminating wasteful spending would be the first step in restoring economic freedom and individual prosperity. Decentralization—shifting power away from Ottawa and back to provinces and municipalities—could help restore local autonomy and limit the federal government's overreach.

Reclaiming National Sovereignty

Canada's policies are dictated more by international bodies like the UN and WEF than by the will of its own people. Exiting destructive agreements, reclaiming control over immigration policy, and prioritizing domestic industries over globalist economic models would be essential in reestablishing national independence.

Restoring Economic and Energy Independence

Rebuilding Canada's economy means unleashing its resource sector, restoring manufacturing, and ending government interference in energy production. Eliminating carbon taxes, deregulating key industries, and investing in self-sufficient energy infrastructure would allow Canada to produce its own wealth rather than relying on foreign imports and ideological environmental policies that cripple national productivity.

Breaking the State-Media Complex

Legacy media's reliance on government funding has turned it into a propaganda machine rather than an independent press. Ending media subsidies and creating financial transparency laws that expose corporate and government influence over the press would allow for a revival of genuine journalism. A truly free press is necessary for an informed and engaged public.

Restoring Free Speech and Individual Liberties

Trudeau's online censorship laws, financial deplatforming, and ever-expanding hate speech regulations have eroded free expression in Canada. Repealing laws that criminalize speech, removing government control over online content, and reinforcing constitutional protections would be necessary to restore an open society where dissenting views are not punished.

Ending the Culture of Dependency

Government expansion has created a population that relies on state handouts rather than self-sufficiency. Welfare reform that prioritizes work incentives rather than permanent dependency would help restore a culture of personal responsibility. Lowering taxes, reducing business regulations, and encouraging entrepreneurship would enable individuals to reclaim control over their own economic futures.

Realigning the Education System

The indoctrination happening in schools and universities is not accidental. Replacing activist-driven curricula with classical education, reinforcing critical thinking over ideological programming, and decentralizing school boards would help break the cycle of state-controlled thought. Encouraging alternative education paths—such as trade schools, apprenticeships, and home-schooling—would empower students with real skills rather than ideological rhetoric.

The Harsh Reality: Is It Too Late?

For all the solutions that exist, there remains one looming question: Is Canada already too far gone? The level of institutional decay, cultural apathy, and economic mismanagement suggests that meaningful change may no longer be possible within the current system. The bureaucracy will not dismantle itself. Politicians will not relinquish their control. And the majority of Canadians, having been conditioned to accept government overreach as normal, may not be willing to resist.

History has shown that once a society becomes fully dependent on the state, reversing that dependency is nearly impossible. Nations that have willingly sacrificed economic freedom, personal liberties, and cultural identity for short-term security rarely find their way back. The collapse may already be inevitable—not in a sudden, catastrophic way, but in the slow erosion of everything that once made Canada a prosperous and independent nation.

If there is a path forward, it will not come from within the system, but from those willing to build something outside of it. The only real solution may be for individuals to prepare for a future where self-reliance, community-building, and parallel institutions replace the crumbling structures of a failing state. The question is no longer whether Canada can be saved, but whether enough people recognize the need to create something new before it's too late.

Is There a Path to Reversing the Collapse, or Is the Damage Too Far Gone?

The collapse of a nation is rarely reversed. History tells us that once a country reaches a tipping point—where corruption is systemic, institutions are weaponized against the people, and economic decline is intentional rather than accidental—it is difficult, if not impossible, to restore what was lost. Canada is now at such a crossroads. The question is not whether the country is in decline, but whether there is a way back, or if the damage is irreversible.

For those who still hold hope, the path to reversing Canada's collapse would require a radical departure from the status quo. Incremental reforms will not fix a system that has been designed to entrench power in the hands of bureaucratic elites and globalist interests. The country's trajectory can only be changed by dismantling the very structures that are accelerating its downfall.

Dismantling the Bureaucratic State

Canada's government has grown too large, too expensive, and too intrusive. Cutting government size, slashing regulations, and eliminating wasteful spending would be the first step in restoring economic freedom and individual prosperity. Decentralization—shifting power away from Ottawa and back to provinces and municipalities—could help restore local autonomy and limit the federal government's overreach.

Reclaiming National Sovereignty

Canada's policies are dictated more by international bodies like the UN and WEF than by the will of its own people. Exiting destructive agreements, reclaiming control over immigration policy, and prioritizing domestic industries over globalist economic models would be essential in reestablishing national independence.

Restoring Economic and Energy Independence

Rebuilding Canada's economy means unleashing its resource sector, restoring manufacturing, and ending government interference in energy production. Eliminating carbon taxes, deregulating key industries, and investing in self-sufficient energy infrastructure would allow Canada to produce its own wealth rather than relying on foreign imports and ideological environmental policies that cripple national productivity.

Breaking the State-Media Complex

Legacy media's reliance on government funding has turned it into a propaganda machine rather than an independent press. Ending media subsidies and creating financial transparency laws that expose corporate and government influence over the press would allow for a revival of genuine journalism. A truly free press is necessary for an informed and engaged public.

Restoring Free Speech and Individual Liberties

Trudeau's online censorship laws, financial deplatforming, and ever-expanding hate speech regulations have eroded free expression in Canada. Repealing laws that criminalize speech, removing government control over online content, and reinforcing constitutional protections would be necessary to restore an open society where dissenting views are not punished.

Ending the Culture of Dependency

Government expansion has created a population that relies on state handouts rather than self-sufficiency. Welfare reform that prioritizes work incentives rather than permanent dependency would help restore a culture of personal responsibility. Lowering taxes, reducing business regulations, and encouraging entrepreneurship would enable individuals to reclaim control over their own economic futures.

Realigning the Education System

The indoctrination happening in schools and universities is not accidental. Replacing activist-driven curricula with classical education, reinforcing critical thinking over ideological programming, and decentralizing school boards would help break the cycle of state-controlled thought. Encouraging alternative education paths—such as trade schools, apprenticeships, and homeschooling—would empower students with real skills rather than ideological rhetoric.

The Harsh Reality: Is It Too Late?

For all the solutions that exist, there remains one looming question: Is Canada already too far gone? The level of institutional decay, cultural apathy, and economic mismanagement suggests that meaningful change may no longer be possible within the current system. The bureaucracy will not dismantle itself. Politicians will not relinquish their control. And the majority of Canadians, having been conditioned to accept government overreach as normal, may not be willing to resist.

History has shown that once a society becomes fully dependent on the state, reversing that dependency is nearly impossible. Nations that have willingly sacrificed economic freedom, personal liberties, and cultural identity for short-term security rarely find their way back. The collapse may already be inevitable—not in a sudden, catastrophic way, but in the slow erosion of everything that once made Canada a prosperous and independent nation.

If there is a path forward, it will not come from within the system, but from those willing to build something outside of it. The only real solution may be for individuals to prepare for a future where self-reliance, community-building, and parallel institutions replace the crumbling structures of a failing state. The question is no longer whether Canada can be saved, but whether enough people recognize the need to create something new before it's too late.

Strategies for Self-Reliance in a Failing State

If the decline of Canada is inevitable, then survival will depend on self-reliance, adaptability, and the ability to operate outside the collapsing system. Individuals and communities must take proactive steps to reduce dependence on government-controlled institutions and instead build resilience through localized and de-centralized alternatives.

Economic Independence

·   Diversify income sources: Relying on a single employer or government assistance leaves individuals vulnerable to economic collapse. Developing multiple streams of income—freelancing, skilled trades, or entrepreneurship—provides greater stability.

·   Invest in hard assets: Savings held in fiat currency are at risk due to inflation and financial deplatforming. Investing in tangible assets like land, tools, precious metals, or even barterable goods ensures long-term security.

·   Support parallel economies: Engaging in local trade networks, private barter systems, and decentralized marketplaces reduces reliance on corporate monopolies and government-controlled supply chains.

Food and Energy Security

·   Grow your own food: Whether through homesteading, urban gardening, or community-supported agriculture, producing your own food mitigates the impact of rising grocery costs and supply chain failures.

·   Develop energy independence: Reducing reliance on govern-ment-controlled energy grids through solar power, wood stoves, or local energy cooperatives ensures autonomy in times of scarcity or policy-induced shortages.

· Store essentials: Having long-term food storage, access to clean water, and essential medical supplies protects against systemic failures and emergency situations.

Community and Mutual Aid Networks

· Build strong local relationships: Government reliance thrives on individual isolation. Strengthening ties with neighbors, small businesses, and community groups ensures mutual support in times of crisis.

· Create skill-sharing networks: Learning essential skills—carpentry, mechanics, first aid, food preservation—empowers individuals and strengthens communal resilience.

· Form independent security structures: As law enforcement becomes increasingly politicized, local communities must be prepared to safeguard their own homes and neighborhoods.

Resisting Digital and Financial Control

· Use decentralized currencies: Cryptocurrencies, local exchange systems, and precious metals offer alternatives to government-controlled digital payment systems.

· Minimize digital surveillance: Using encrypted communication, avoiding state-backed ID programs, and limiting exposure to data-harvesting platforms protects privacy and autonomy.

· Resist financial dependency: Reducing reliance on government benefits or corporate-controlled financial services ensures that individuals cannot be economically coerced into compliance.

Reclaiming Cultural and Intellectual Independence

· Educate outside the system: Homeschooling, alternative schooling, and community-led education programs prevent state indoctrination and preserve critical thinking skills.

· Support independent media: Consuming and funding non-state-controlled news sources ensures access to truthful information.

· Preserve history and traditions: Recognizing and valuing national heritage strengthens cultural identity and resilience against ideological programming.

Self-reliance is not just about survival—it is about reclaiming personal sovereignty in a system designed to strip individuals of their autonomy. As Canada moves further toward centralized control, those who build alternative structures will be the ones best positioned to thrive in the aftermath of institutional collapse.

51st State? The Quiet Integration of Canada into the American Empire

For decades, Canada has prided itself on maintaining a distinct identity from the United States, clinging to a sense of sovereignty that, in reality, has been steadily eroding. While Canadians are quick to dismiss the idea of their nation becoming America's 51st state, the reality is that, in many ways, it already functions as one—economically, politically, and culturally. The question is not whether Canada is being absorbed into the American empire, but rather if this slow-motion annexation is by design, and if so, who benefits?

Economic Dependence and the Illusion of Independence

Canada's economy is deeply intertwined with that of the United States. Over 75% of Canadian exports go directly to the U.S., and much of Canada's financial infrastructure is directly influenced by the Federal Reserve's monetary policies. While Canadian politicians claim to pursue independent economic strategies, the reality is that Canadian fiscal and monetary decisions are often reactionary to American interests rather than proactive national policies.

With the steady deindustrialization of Canada, reliance on American goods has skyrocketed. Canada imports most of its manufactured goods from the U.S. while exporting raw resources like oil, lumber, and minerals—mimicking the economic dynamic of a resource colony rather than an independent nation. Recent policies have further entrenched this dependency, as restrictions on do-

THE GREAT CANADIAN COLLAPSE

mestic energy production force Canada to rely more heavily on American refineries and global supply chains.

The USMCA trade agreement (NAFTA 2.0) only solidified this one-sided relationship, placing Canada in an economic position where it must comply with American trade regulations or risk devastating economic repercussions. At this point, Canada's economic fate is largely dictated by Washington, not Ottawa.

Political Subordination and the End of Sovereignty

Despite presenting itself as an independent democracy, Canada's government increasingly operates as a satellite of the U.S. political establishment. Foreign policy is dictated by Washington, as seen in Canada's unquestioning alignment with American-led military interventions, sanctions, and geopolitical maneuvering.

The Five Eyes intelligence alliance ensures that Canadian surveillance operations are deeply intertwined with U.S. national security interests. Canadian intelligence agencies often act in lockstep with their American counterparts, raising concerns about whether Canada even controls its own security apparatus.

Domestically, the Trudeau government mirrors U.S. progressive politics, importing American culture wars, racial politics, and social policies wholesale. The country's rapid adoption of DEI (Diversity, Equity, and Inclusion) policies, aggressive climate regulations, and digital censorship laws all stem from broader globalist frameworks pushed primarily by the American political and corporate elite.

Cultural Absorption and the Loss of Identity

Canada's cultural independence has all but disappeared. Hollywood, Silicon Valley, and Wall Street dictate what Canadians watch, read, and consume. American media companies dominate the Canadian landscape, shaping national discourse and influencing public opinion far more than any domestic outlets.

Meanwhile, legacy media in Canada, despite being heavily subsidized by the federal government, often takes its cues from U.S.

narratives. Political movements, social debates, and ideological battles in Canada largely mirror American discourse, demonstrating the extent to which Canadian identity is now an extension of American cultural hegemony.

Even on a demographic level, Canada's mass immigration policies are increasingly resembling those of the United States—importing large populations without integrating them into a distinct national culture, further eroding any cohesive Canadian identity.

The Endgame: A Formal Merger?

While outright political annexation may not be on the immediate horizon, Canada's slow but steady absorption into the American sphere suggests that full integration—whether through economic dependency, political alignment, or cultural assimilation—is already happening. The real question is whether Canadians are even aware that their sovereignty is being systematically dismantled.

Would Canadians even resist the idea of becoming the 51st state? With a failing economy, increasing taxation, and a government more focused on globalist agendas than national prosperity, some might see integration with the U.S. as a better option than remaining under the bureaucratic chokehold of Ottawa. In the coming years, Canada may have to decide whether to attempt to reclaim its sovereignty or simply accept its status as America's most polite subsidiary.

CONCLUSION

The Crossroads of Collapse and Rebirth
Canada stands at a defining moment in its history. The nation that once thrived on self-reliance, economic prosperity, and individual freedom is now burdened by systemic corruption, government overreach, and a population increasingly dependent on the state. Whether through economic mismanagement, ideological subversion, or deliberate sabotage by globalist elites, the collapse of Canada is not a future possibility—it is already happening in slow motion.

The question is no longer whether the country is failing, but what comes next?

If the current trajectory continues, Canada will devolve further into a bureaucratic wasteland, where personal freedoms are sacrificed for the illusion of security, where productivity is replaced by state dependency, and where the ruling class tightens its grip over an increasingly powerless population. The institutions that once safeguarded the nation's stability—education, media, law, and economy—have been repurposed to enforce compliance rather than foster resilience. The only certainty in this model is continued decline.

But collapse is not the only possible outcome. Rebirth is still an option—for those who are willing to reject the system that led us here. Throughout history, nations that have suffered similar fates have sometimes found a way to break free. The answer has never come from political saviors, government intervention, or external forces—it has always come from those who refused to submit, who built new systems outside of the old, and who reclaimed personal and collective sovereignty by force of will.

The path forward for Canadians who refuse to be ruled by corruption and incompetence is clear:

- Reject dependency—financial, ideological, and political.
- Build parallel systems—in economics, education, and community security.
- Decentralize power—shifting influence away from Ottawa and into the hands of local, self-sufficient networks.
- Take control of information—supporting independent media and resisting state propaganda.
- Embrace self-reliance—economically, intellectually, and culturally.

History is written by those who take action. If Canada is to have a future beyond managed decline, it will not be rebuilt by those in power—it will be reclaimed by those who refuse to let their country become a failed state.

The time for passivity is over. The collapse is already here. The only question that remains is whether enough Canadians are willing to break free from the system before there is nothing left to save.

BIBLIOGRAPHY

This book draws on a combination of historical analysis, economic data, political events, and investigative research to outline the trajectory of Canada's decline. The following sources, reports, and references have informed the arguments and conclusions presented:

Government Reports & Economic Data

· Bank of Canada Reports – Inflation trends, monetary policy, and economic forecasting.

· Statistics Canada – Economic, demographic, and social trends affecting the nation.

· Parliamentary Budget Officer Reports – Federal debt, taxation, and government spending analysis.

· Canada Mortgage and Housing Corporation (CMHC) – Housing crisis, real estate market trends.

· Office of the Auditor General of Canada – Government accountability and spending inefficiencies.

International Organizations & Policy Documents

· United Nations (UN) Sustainable Development Goals & Agenda

2030 – Impact on Canadian policy.

· World Economic Forum (WEF) Publications – 'The Great Reset' and global governance initiatives.

· International Monetary Fund (IMF) & World Bank Reports – Canadian economic vulnerabilities and globalist economic frameworks.

· World Trade Organization (WTO) Agreements – Trade policies and economic sovereignty.

Legislation & Policy Papers

· Bill C-11 (Online Streaming Act) – Censorship laws and digital media control.

· Bill C-18 (Online News Act) – Government funding of media and influence over narratives.

· Canada's Carbon Tax Framework – The economic impact of climate policies.

· USMCA Trade Agreement – Canadian economic integration with the U.S.

· Federal Budget Documents – Expenditure reports, debt accumulation, and taxation policies.

Books & Academic Works

· Friedman, Milton – Capitalism and Freedom (1962) – Economic principles on free markets and government intervention.

· Hayek, Friedrich – The Road to Serfdom (1944) – The dangers of centralized control and the erosion of freedom.

· Orwell, George – 1984 (1949) – Parallels between authoritarian control and modern government overreach.

· Rand, Ayn – Atlas Shrugged (1957) – The consequences of overregulation, collectivism, and economic sabotage.

· Bezmenov, Yuri – Love Letter to America (1984) – Soviet subversion tactics and their application in Western decline.

Investigative Journalism & Reports

· Financial Post & National Post – Analysis of government policies, taxation, and economic trends.

- Blacklock's Reporter – In-depth coverage of government corruption and legislative overreach.
- Rebel News & True North – Independent media investigating censorship and media bias.
- Globe and Mail & Toronto Sun – Select reports on economic policy and government accountability.

Alternative & Independent Research

- The Democracy Index (The Economist) – Canada's ranking in global democratic assessments.
- Fraser Institute Reports – Economic freedom, taxation, and public policy impact analysis.
- Macdonald-Laurier Institute – Independent policy research on governance and sovereignty.
- Jordan Peterson Lectures & Essays – Psychological and ideological insights on cultural decay.

9 781998 704569